THE GREATER PURPOSE

Book Two: The Purpose Trilogy

PURPOSE

Answers the Age-Old Question —

Why Am I Here?

Robyn G. Locke

Given by the Elders

The Original Purpose:
Answers the Age-Old Question — Why Am I Here?
Published by Golden Page Publishing
Atlanta, GA
Copyright ©2020 Robyn G. Locke. All rights reserved.

No part of this book may be reproduced in any form or
by any mechanical means, including information storage
and retrieval systems without permission in writing from
the publisher/author, except by a reviewer who may quote
passages in a review.

All images, logos, quotes, and trademarks included in this
book are subject to use according to trademark and copyright
laws of the United States of America.

ISBN: 978-0-9992458-5-9 (Amazon)
ISBN: 979-8-9877542-6-9 (Ingram)
ISBN: 979-8-9877542-7-6 (ebook)

BODY, MIND & SPIRIT / Inspiration & Personal Growth

QUANTITY PURCHASES: Schools, companies,
professional groups, clubs, and other organizations may
qualify for special terms when ordering quantities of this title.
Email info@AdvancedEnergetics.org for more details.

All rights reserved by Robyn G. Locke and
Golden Page Publishing.
This book is printed in the United States of America.

Table of Contents

In Appreciation

I cannot imagine life without the Love, support, and guidance of the Elders. I am in constant awe of their words, the Loving energy they emit, and the new insights they allow me to glean. In sharing from their unique vantage, my perspectives in life have changed accordingly. They are my most valued and treasured resource, lifeline, gift. They are the reason I can't wait for each day to unfold as I discover something wonderful and previously unknown. It is for my unique purpose that I strive for more to be. It is the allness in all that I do as I seek to be and discover more.

I am grateful for my Mother. In life, she was a spiritual trailblazer. She continually sought to discover more. She never accepted a status quo sort of existence, nor did she limit how she sought to understand more. Growing up, she was my spiritual role model and mentor. Mom physically passed, making her transition earlier this year. I appreciate her unabashed desire to look beyond the more rigid belief system which existed during my early youth as she sought to discover more.

A special thank you to Lorie, Lorna, Victoria, and Polly, who have brought *The Original Purpose* book into form, as it is now affixed and made real.

Preamble

We know, oftentimes, that to move into uncharted waters is difficult and sometimes seems entered into with a degree of trepidation. Know that as we continue further, there may be steps within this process that uncover a pathway you are meant to become aware of in this lifetime today.

And so we do say to engage all from the measure of Love as this is the measure we seek to connect you with this day. For in this discovery and all that is to be given, know that above all else, you are deeply Loved. Universe, Source, all that elicits a posture of how you came to be here in this space in time, do continue to support you and each of your endeavors.

Always know this is the truth behind each measure, each step, each understanding that does evolve from this space (moving) forward. We give this as we move now to continue.

Preface

So often, in the formulation of life, there is not the full understanding of what coming to Earth, incarnating here and being a part of the flow of all that is in existence when one is physically placed. And so know that as you have chosen to reside in the consciousness and the densities of this Earth platform, you had made the election to do so. You had made the election because you wanted to understand something you could not (understand) in any other way. It was from this premise that the possibility and endless potential of what this Earth experience might express itself to be. It was this, then, that caused you to move into physical form and begin the rounds of incarnation here.

Often, there is not the full understanding of knowing that life flows differently here (on Earth) than when one is in spiritual flow. The densities here are expressed as they are for a unique purpose. And that unique purpose is so that you might more fully know how thus and such feels. For isn't it the feeling that gives you the understanding of the quality of what is or is not preferred?

We will say that there is an aspect that is not fully known when there is the posturing of preference to incarnate here.

And by this we mean, that it is not fully understood, the full weightiness of what the uniqueness of this Earth plane does evoke and allow one to feel. And it is in the feeling component where so much more can be understood. So that when each lifetime is complete, there is an energetic accounting of what occurred.

The gifts, and those qualities which have been established to become known, are then uniquely those that are qualities imbued by the Soul Essence. And the Soul ultimately seeks for all of its known accomplishments, all of these known qualities, to be reabsorbed when the being that is incarnate recognizes that there are gifts to be claimed.

And the value to the being, or personality, or the one in existence to claim these things, is that they do not need to be, at this point, redeveloped. In other words, you do not need to do them all over again, for they are already the property and owner-ship of the Soul Essence. It is merely in the recognition that you seek to reintegrate that which is of its rightful owner. For you see, Soul Essence seeks the totality of the wholeness which it does seek to incorpo-rate into its being and world.

And so when the incarnation is the last one, then there is the preference to draw all those gifts in so that the wholeness might become known. And the value for the personality or the one living the life, to claim those, does give a fuller measure of ability to the one who has not yet estab-lished the right to do so any other way.

How to Receive to Perceive

This book will enable an inner discovery and personal transformation to occur. Might you begin your engagement here when you are ready to be in that contemplative or meditative sort of way? Engage by enlisting one of our many meditations to set the mood. This will enable you to enjoy a frequency adjustment. This adjustment is the best means for a receptivity to occur and for our insights to be more readily perceived and received.

As we move forward in Light and Love, know that all is a matter of acceptance when it is time for you to do so. Might you be in that space now? Be in that space where the mental box does not reside, and there is an allowing of all that is to progress this day.

Having placed the mental box upon the shelf — locked it, blocked it, we now seek to allow more to move into that mental space that was once occupied by something with a sheer knowingness. But today, there is that opportunity for more. And so enlist and move this day to absorb, and expand, and calibrate, and be all that you were intended to be in this lifetime, as you embrace more. And so, we move to discuss something of deep importance and something that ...

We do want you to know
That all is in the mix of flow.
When you are reverent and willing to know
What more might be awaiting and bestowed.

For now through Light and Love we do progress
To give to you all that we now profess.
And it is in this measure that we describe
That all is given in Love,
For it is in Love where we do reside.

Let us travel this road of discovery together as we embark and provide how each tomorrow might become more effortless. In this way, each new day will seek to reveal more of what you desire to be made tangible and real.

Now you will have the means to enact and bring
about all you seek to come ... into being.

Stepping into

Chapter 1

Transition

Do you recognize that often there are subtleties underway and underfoot, subtleties that will lead you to the path of your preference or perhaps something else? We would say as you move, you do so with purpose. But when you move listlessly, or you move without a preferred agenda or objective in your future, then how do you move from here to there effectively?

And so we would say when one transitions, they move into an altered space. Altered in that it is not as it is when physically placed. We would say when one is physically placed, there is more of a definition of the time in space in which they reside … physically.

As you move out of the body and into that transitory time, in between embodiments, there is not the anchoring one might feel while earthbound. And so, it is more of an illusionary premise. Although we would say when you are in that space, it does feel most vivid and real. And it does feel as if you know all that you need to know because in this space, you are anchored further with the understanding of what you knew before.

What you believed while physically placed is what you are reinforced with during this time. And so all the different perceptions you held while in the body are anchored and reinforced when out of the body. And so in this time and in this space, there is the illusionary premise that there is an all-knowingness in that existence.

And we will tell you this is illusionary because when you come from here to there, Earth to transition, you are reinforced by all you knew while physically placed. And so there is the aha moment that does transcend all time because, during this experience, you are anchored with what you knew to be true, thought to be true, believed to be true. And perhaps it was, or perhaps it was not.

And so we would say while feet are firmly planted on this Earth, to do all you can to enlist measures. And to do those things that will further reinforce a know-ingness but not from the posture of the mind and not from the posture of ego.

For when the mind and ego lay siege on what must become known, and if there is a tinge of inner validation, an inner awareness that is not aligned as it might be when it is more placed toward egoic measure or mind stimulation, and not anchored initially from the heart and the heart center, then you may have an under-standing that may be adrift of what truly is.

When you transition, you move into a space of being given reinforcement of what was believed before. In that space as one does move to progress and adopt what is to occur within a subsequent lifetime, there is not the questioning, there is not the wonderment, nor the understanding of what knowing something else might elicit.

And so we would say it does alter all that does pass and move beyond this time. For it is the structuring, and the planning, and the doing of the objective to prepare for the next step … to prepare for the next embodiment. To get all the ducks in a row, so to speak, so as you move to embody once again, you embody with a premise devised from this time.

And there may be individuals who

energetically align and aspire to move into different arenas as well. And you and they do confer and are aligned to move an objective forward. Perhaps there is a belief that to experience this or that may yield a preferred understanding. But we would say that at this time, there is so much illusion in the midst of it all, that there is no longer the plotting and planning toward the original mission and toward the original objective. Although there is a component of one to the other, there is not the underlying and broad-based understanding that had come before.

With the original purpose, there is so much more that was comprised within that so that the fuller measure, the fuller understanding, the energetic component which comprised all these various nuances brought to a head. And so there is in many regards a minimization, a minimizing of what was understood, what might be understood, and what might be enacted.

And when one considers that many have lived from an oppressive state and are oppressed mentally, they then move into this transitory time and do not have the full scope of *all is possible*. There is a miniaturization and almost an inability to think from a grander regard. To move into more of a broad-based perspective of what might be understood were it to be deployed and employed.

In this transitory time, there is a moving from this to that, and then onto something else before the next embodiment is yet to occur. And so we would say to elicit questions during this time. Elicit multiple questions and ask for more to be given. Do not be directed so easily. For when one stops to inquire, when one stops to ask or elicit more, then there is the possibility for more to enter in.

We would say to linger in all regards. And to not move swiftly from here to there. And to pause. And to contemplate. And to move in less illusionary but more realistic terms by calling forth those who did reinforce your life while physically placed, for they are still accessible at this time. For in many regards, they are with you from lifetime to lifetime, and know your struggle, know your accomplishments, and know your objectives.

It is the disconnect from these ones,

and the disconnect from the greater premise and greater purpose, that does often allow less to be known. And we seek for the maximization, for the full incorporation, for the alignment of the one to become known more fully. So then when they move, and they enlist to do more, they can do more from a broad-based perspective. They can do and accomplish more in a more uplifted manner. They can do and set about to set intentions so those who would buoy them up instead of envisioning something of a lower nature, hoping there would be a realization from that lower space to one of greater precipice.

And we would say it is the posturing and planning and doing so without enlisting guidance. For there is guidance, but you have greater guidance that is accessible, that is available, that is all about you even in this transitory time.

And so we would encourage one to the other, to move from the space of wanting to know more, wanting to enlist all the tools that are available. And those tools are available upon your call and your recognition of wanting more (and) of asking and enlisting assistance.

When this does happen, when there is the true calling forth of that which will enable you to know more, to do more, to be more in a subsequent time for the plotting and planning will be done in a more measured way, and will be done in a more uplifted way, and will be done in a way where there are dynamics brought into play that will be of a more significant nature.

For you see, many that are within the Earth premise today live meagerly and do not feel that there is the expanse within Universe to provide more. Do not feel the abundance from which Universe does exist and offer each within the round of incarnations. And so there is almost an aspect of not believing there is enough to go around.

And we tell you this is not so. And so when you are in that proposed arena, that area of illusionary wonder, remember this — remember when you ask, more is given. And when you call forth those who are Stewards of your lifestream, those who are Guardians of you, those who are watchers of what you are doing, they await your asking. They await your questioning. They await your wonderment of why they are there and that you even recognize that they are there. For often, they can be so close but yet so far away because there is not the recognition of who they are within the dynamic of the day.

When you move into a transitory position, remember, *if nothing else*, to ask that all be given that would move you back to your original purpose. Move you back to your original objective for embodying on this physical plane, on this Earth plane. By merely asking, you will open up a dynamic of what more might be given and known so these things exist with an understanding of all that might be. And that there might be a higher vibrational way to attune and to glean more from the existence from which they will soon be within.

And so we move to the next step, but we do want you to understand within this transitory time that there is much to be gleaned. There is much to be understood, but it is to be recognized that it is not as vivid and as actual as you may believe when in that space. For as we have said, it is an illusionary posture in that time and space.

If you will embrace that and know that it is a reinforcement of many things that are or are not so, then you will move into that space with a greater understanding and knowingness of what might be given, what might be offered, and how you might move into the next round of incarnation.

Behind the Scenes

In the backspace, in the backdrop, in the behind-the-scenes of activities that exist within your heritage, within the past that you intrinsically have known before, each pathway does elicit a purpose. For as you step into the knowingness and becoming the awareness of the purpose that you did initiate, that you did plant the earlier seeds to allow the growing and cultivation of the awareness of that activity or thing, it is more specifically the energy that you sought to understand. And in understanding the energetic component that was amiss and lacking from your current awareness, was to know more deeply how something felt.

And so that is the true navigator, do you see, within this life and any other.

And even in the in-between state, there is always the movement. There is always the proclivity to understand and know something more deeply than could have been known without it.

And so during this in-between time, there is a request, a solicitation, a need to move from this space into the next. And we would say it is an ushering in of the elective process of moving to reincarnate yet again.

And we have said this is an illusionary time, for it is. For much is met in a way that is presupposed and allowed to occur in the existence of time, yet you might believe you have the option to move in one way or the other. And, of course, you do. But it is not seen as such, and it is more of a melding to move from one space to the next. To move into incarnation, once again, as if it were always presupposed, or already presupposed, that you would do so.

As you move to incarnate, there are those that come and ask for you to go about setting up your next life intention. There is an original intention that could be attached to here if it were known to be in existence. But at this point, there is not the awareness or understanding that the original purpose does exist.

And so there is more of an alignment with the premise that does surface at this point, which is a component of the greater, larger, more vast purpose. It is a component but not the entire understanding of what is. And so you move to embrace, understand, and add degrees of endeavor to it.

You add or facilitate that understanding in a greater way. And these others do come. So there is a community of sorts that are enlisted to facilitate what you could not perhaps do on your own. And these others are ready, and there are various levels of discussion to anticipate how one might meet and a feeling that is evoked. And an understanding that is given so more might be understood when you and they are physically placed. This occurs for a time, and they are enmeshed and melded into the fabric of the next life experience.

And so we will say there is the free will component, which is a part of this process and continues throughout each step, whether in the physical form or within the transitory one. For at each point, there is the opportunity to ask for more — to ask for a deeper understanding, to ask for more components, to ask for other players, to ask for something that resonates more deeply or is more purposeful. But oftentimes, this does not happen. And so the elements of this next life are given. And this process is moved through with a degree of not only specificity but a uniqueness and a clarity of choice.

As we look at this a bit more, let us say that there is not the engagement nor the willingness to shift from this to that. It is almost in the knowingness of what has come to pass, and what is lying at one's feet and what you are moving to enact, and do, and be in this next round, is more specifically understood.

And we ask if this is the purpose for which you understood? For there is an interpretation in this portion of the transitory time. An interpretation that all is known. But you see, all is not known. And only a component of what is known is actually utilized to put this next life plan into play.

We will say there is a compartmentalization. There is a limitation in that the understanding of what one is utilizing during this time is not as it is. It is not as the Soul Essence believes it to be. And so this is a degree of a limitation that is not recognized, not understood for the illusionary premise that is in play. And so oftentimes, there are components inserted and added that layer degrees of difficulty into the life path of the one who is to live this life in an uplifted sort of way.

For you see, when there is the need to make things a bit more difficult, to show how one can rise above the difficulty. How one can move beyond what is almost as if being in quicksand; there is not the ability to step up. There is not the need to move to this or that in a way that might be more uplifted, for there is almost a proving that one can access or reach a level that is most illusionary. For when one believes they have found it, they are ready to cast to the wind that which might propel them in a way that would allow them to navigate and reach their goal in a more illumined way.

So perhaps this is the area that is most foggy. For the premise it supposes is that all will be accomplished even with these added dynamics. But do you see when one has come from a difficult life and is heavy-laden, there is now the understanding that life is difficult and heavy-laden?

And so when the planning does occur again, there is the added layering which occurs that is most unnecessary. We share this component, so should you get to this space again, you choose differently. That through awareness now of that space, that you choose for it to be a more uplifted and easier next life, that you do not add in difficulty or some strategic move that would cause a layering aspect to be in play. Or more dramas to be undertaken. Or more scenarios to be engulfed by this one or that, that would delay, and insert so many different choices that it is most difficult to determine what one is to do at that crossroad.

So we ask for the next steps to be measured. We ask for consideration of the next steps to be, in a manner of speaking, simpler. And for more abundant-type scenarios to be introduced so the life isn't laden with lack, for there are many who know more lack than they do prosperity. And we seek to minimize this if nothing else. We seek to minimize this part of the equation so there is more beauty and light brought into this world, rather than the adversity that seems to be moving about this space today.

And so as there is the movement forward into the incarnation of the next life, various components are gathered and entered in. They are considerations, and they are contemplations, and they are activities and individuals who will line the way and be noted for what they interject into the next experience. And so all are a means of navigation. All are a means of a knowingness for which pathway to take when that person discussed a topic that has a recollection of memory that moves one to select this or that over another option.

Recognize each thing introduced does serve a purpose. And it is to connect the one with the other so a certain experience is rendered and felt.

In the In-Between Time

In the in-between time before the embodiment is known, whether it is the first, second, third, or some successive time in the future, there is the in-between time in which many do postulate and formulate what this existence is to be. And how it is. And what does occur when preparing for another round of incarnation, or perhaps the first incarnation.

We would say now, let us now focus on one who has embodied before and is in that in-between posture and moving to incarnate yet again. We would say within this time period, there is much activity. There is, of course, the reinforcement of all that has come before. So let us say all that you have known and believed in the life you have just left does remain firmly intact as the belief system that you carry forward into this next round. And this is the in-between, transitory state in which we discuss. What does occur in this platform of awareness?

When you step into this portal, you are then greeted by all you have known before or you feel energetically aligned to. And they do formulate and flow with you to reinforce the measures of understanding that were gleaned in the lifetime previously held. And so all does move in the manner of concurrence with what was and is within the belief system that grew from the awareness of the previous incarnation; all the platforms and understandings, as they were believed to have existed, now get that confirmation that they were as was believed.

We tell you that free will choice is a real thing. And when you freely choose to embrace this or that understanding, it is not to be done lightly. It is to be done from the premise and the posture that this is a most important thing. And it is to be held in a most sacred way. For when you take on a belief, you do then limit the potentiality of any other belief that is in concurrence or opposition to the belief held.

For you see, when the belief is adopted, it has certain tenants or understandings that allow it to postulate and formulate as it might. And so we will say to look upon beliefs in a most serious way. For in that, you recognize how all that might be chosen, was not. For this one thing was what rose to the surface. And so to cast it aside in this in-between, transitory time would not be of the posture that Universe,

Source Energy, would enlist. For to do so would be, in a manner of speaking, diminishing the free will component that led you there. And so why would Universe, Source Energy, or that Greater Power, seek to diminish what you have chosen to embrace, accept ... believe?

And so in this in-between time, when beliefs are held as they are, there is then that reinforcement of the belief. The belief then is held to the higher calibre and the higher standard of equality and the equation that you have attributed to it. And so others come to reinforce that, and these beliefs are seen to be validated. But we will say, as we have said before, that this is an illusionary time. And so what you believe to be firmly affixed, firmly in place, may not be that way at all.

For Universe always seeks to make you correct in all that you postulate upon. And so when you look for confirmation of this or that, and you receive what you believe to be a sign that this or that is as you believed it to be, then you move on as you accept what is. But we would say to linger upon the premise. To linger upon the premise and to look beyond the limitation of the mind and the limitation of the egoic stance, which likes the confirmation and the validity of the rightness of choice.

And so there is a discernment that is underfoot, we would say. There is a discernment that is most necessary for you to ... see. And that is the mind, ego, that chatter that goes on incessantly does seek confirmation of what it needs to know. But have you then ever considered to take what you postulate upon and muse upon it? Contemplate upon it in meditation. For it is in the contemplative moments when the small voice, the meek and mild voice, the voice that is not reactionary but does move to support, but in a more long-term sort of way. Not in the reactionary way that ego might employ. And so, might you look again? Look again at all the choices, all the belief systems, or perhaps the most important ones as the others will rise to the surface in their appropriate time.

In this transitory time, there is then the posturing of the beliefs, the buoying up of them, and those that are sent or that arrive as a means of confirmation of all that has been contemplated on before. And so then one does move to structure out the next lifetime. And the next lifetime may be in a few short years or maybe in decades or beyond. It is the preference, and perhaps, too, it is sometimes the posturing of the enlightenment of the one who does make the preference from a more quizzical standpoint of wanting to know more of what is.

We will say that to engage in what is believed to be truth and a validation of such, it is also the means by which so much more can become known. For here, too, there is an allowing, of asking — of asking to discover what more might be given. But you see, if you believe you already know, then there is no point to ask, for the reinforcements are all you sought in the first place. For with the reinforcements is the validation of the belief system that was in existence before.

And so we would say to stop and pause and to elicit to discover more. To call upon Angels, Light Bearers, and those whom you believe worked with you in the Earth plane to now step forward. To assist you in the path that you are moving to engage with once again. And so, seek to call in the reinforcements. Seek to call in those that worked behind-the-scenes while you were physically placed and ask for their intercession. Ask for them to interject into what might be moving forward.

For this is, as we might posture, an illusionary time, but it does not feel that way when in the throws of this most transient time. And so, as you move to do this or that, more is given. You perhaps preface what you would like to understand and know; know that you are moving from the reality from which you did exist before.

In other words, all is not known at this time. And you are not moving with a greater more-expanded awareness to plot and plan your next step. So as you chose to believe within the Earth quadrant, while physically placed, that same belief system has now moved with you from that existence to the next. And so they (your beliefs) are concurrently traveling with you. They are moving from the physical space to the non-physical space. And there is an almost seamless manner in which this or that is understood as it was understood before.

And so there is not the ability to miss a beat. The confirmation is there; the ability to understand and discern what was gleaned before is most certainly the correct posture. And so now you move forward to make that life election in the next incarnation.

And perhaps you are in the posture that you do not believe in reincarnation. It does not resonate for you, and you do not understand how this can be when you know nothing else but this lifetime, as you have lived much of your life mentally. And we would say to move beyond the mental box. We would say to shelf the mind for a time and to recognize that the mental posturings will not get you from here to there. For now (in this space), you do not have the mental box that plays incessantly and the egoic measure that played when physically placed. But now you have simply the knowingness of all you knew before and what is.

Chapter 2

Uncharted Waters

As we begin this next chapter, know we move into uncharted waters, uncharted and unseen for a time. But might you consider that now is the time to move into spaces that were previously unknown? If you continue to simply regurgitate teachings that have been written and rewritten, said and re-said, tried and inspired to achieve a different outcome from a limited set of understandings … well then, you will not progress much further than you have before. But we would say it is time to move in a way that is now inspired to lift up and progress you beyond the current point in which you now reside.

Will you begin by taking deep breaths? In and out. With a purposeful intention to be able to incorporate and integrate that which we share. For in this way, you might be able to ponder upon the words that are given in the Love in which they are instilled and inspired to be conveyed, for we do share this and all information with a Loving intent. A Loving intent that you may know more today than yesterday.

As life moves as it does, know there are postures and premises in play that are within the flow and the mix of the day. And by this we mean that they are crafted and energetically inspired by what is floating and wafting about. And so when there is, and are, postures that are of not the highest frequency, that are of not the highest nature that they might otherwise be inspired from, conspired with, that they might be other-wise attained, the day then shifts to mirror the energy which has collectively accrued.

And so, oftentimes, it is not that there is a pathway set out in stone that these things must occur in thus and such of a manner, but rather it is the choices made by those who are in this Earth embodiment that are there and collectively conspiring to create an energy that allows the movement to proceed as it is aligned to do.

And so we will say if there is a posture that causes the derailing of a more uplifted energy, that causes the breaking down of something that could be buoyed up by the energy that would change almost instantaneously were that different energy to occur, then there is a collective understanding that has drawn a different scenario into play.

It is not that there is an aligned measure to bring forward something that is not preferred into being from a universal posture, but rather the collective energies that are put into play by the ones who are physically placed. And those then do craft what moves forward into their future. Do you see it can be no other way?

Do you see that were there to be an inspired creation that was of a lower nature, we would say, why would Universe create such a pathway for those whom Universe so deeply Loves and wants only the highest and best calling; only the highest and best measure to be enacted within their day?

We would say that the energy created within the mix of the day from those who are aligned to create that energy, they then move that energy out and into being in a way only they can do. Only they then can move this energy to be one way or the other by the thoughts they keep. By the way they align their actions, by the way they instill their activities, and the way they forecast and project what they wish to occur within their being and world and future.

And so, know that each are the creator of their own destiny. And oftentimes, they know it not. For many do not see the fearful enterprise they might hold within a day, or the anxiousness, or perhaps even to say neediness necessitated by one's mental posture, does relegate what does move forward into their future reality. And so it is not that Universe has crafted life to be this way or that way, one way or the other, but rather it is the flow of energy that is created from the one who is postured in the Earth plane at this point in time.

When there is the posturing and the aligning with the negative aspect that is perhaps there but need not be. Need not be fully focused upon or given fuel to accelerate that which could be easily diminished by a different thought, by a different premise, by a different out-picturing, or promise for the day to unfold in a different way. And so we will say that there is not the need for certain things to come to pass, but yet they will most certainly be because that is the focus, that is the energy, that is the direction that is placed upon the activity that is now arising. Arising, one might say, from the ashes as the phoenix.

Arising in the beauty and light of taking something that is mired and not worth bringing forward, and instead bringing forward something of beauty, and light, and purpose. And so it is all how you see things. It is all how you intend for your manifestation, of what you mentally create, to move forward.

But do you see if you were to align and bring forward from the heart center, from that space once anchored and aligned in a more uplifted way, then all the energy and aspirational objectives would be brought forward in a more uplifted and inspired way? Then more might progress in a way that would germinate and generate something of value and of purpose, and aligned in a way that would move not only self but others to a different space at this point in time.

And so release these negative, not wanted feeling energy aspects, and move to align with those things that feel better. Move to align with each of these things in a way that will then uplift your next step. Will move you to be in a space of Love, and purpose, and understanding.

Can you see this is the better option? This is the better way to progress. For then, others can feel your energy, feel your optimism, feel your uplifted beat and measure. And they then can move to resonate like that rather than this.

We ask for you to consider this objective, this day. To move, and shift, and become all that you seek to be inspired from another. For you are to become the inspiration. You are to be the one who does inspire others who seek to emulate what you do, how you have gotten to where you are. And they, then, would like to shift and change into that. And it is all possible by merely redirecting the thoughts and the energy that you keep.

If you will do this one measure, so much more can flow into being this day. And in this way, we do set the anchor. We do set the foundational premise. We do set all we know into motion for the positivity you will evoke and give to mankind with this one undertaking when anchored in Love.

Align, Move Forward and Into Being

As we progress, let us look at the actual entrance into this world of form. Might you know all that does progress from this space is of measure? It is of measure in that it is to enact that one thing which you have presupposed to be the thing that will bring you into alignment with all that is.

And so as you move into Earth, you enter with a wonderment and awe of all that is to befall you; all that is to move into the line of space that is to connect each thing suggested and introduced in this transitory time that you have just passed from. And so this is a passing into the physical stage.

And within this physical time, there is a brief remembering, and then that does fade as well. It is during this time that so much now is being moved into cue, moved into action, moved into the alignment that will direct and allow your steps to be more purposely placed.

But during this time, there is also that forgetfulness that does enter in. Forgetfulness that has been enacted so there is a full understanding from the perspective of free will, and the occurrences of free will that are, in this way, allowed. For with free will, there is so much more to enter in.

But do you see from the transitory time where there was not the recall, there was not the full understanding of the true intent, the true purpose, the true understanding that much has been amiss for a time? It is amiss in that we suggest that there is not the full awareness in the transitory time. And so there is less than that moving into this space.

And so, without the full recall in the transitory time and moving into this space, there is then a lesser-than understanding of what is underfoot. And there is not the full awareness of what is being enacted and what is to be enacted, for there is not the full recall of the full extent of all that was put into play.

And so we suggest now there is not the awareness, not the understanding, not the full jettison of all that might be were you to be in this space from the original incarnation. For that is the closest you will have been in the full alignment of all that might be to enact this more relevant understanding moving forward.

And so what might be done? What might be done when one enters into a life form, and you must now rediscover the things you knew before? And in the rediscovery, there is, in many ways, the feeling that when you connect to that thing that perhaps is not even the aspect that is the truth component that you have discovered before. When you find that once again, there is a familiar feel, there is an aha moment that you have aligned with that thing you've been in search of for so very long.

But when the aha moment is not what it was meant to elicit, was not the full extent of understanding you were meant to glean, was not all it might have been once before, when that is rediscovered, and you believe you have now found that thing which was most prevalent, well then, what has it moved you to believe?

And we suggest it has moved you to believe something that was less-than, something that was not quite it, and now you have nestled into that premise, that concept, that belief pattern once again.

And so, how to shake that? How to

shake that thing which is so seemingly important now? And we would say to do a subconscious reset where you release and relinquish so many things that are burdensome and are not as they were meant to be intrinsically understood.

We say to release them through this process so you might move differently. So you might embrace things from a higher calibre, a different calibre, a calibre more aligned with where you sought to be in this embodiment, where you sought to be in this way, where you sought to know and understand … more.

For you see, you came to understand how in this physical plane you would feel when enacting this thing that you did not fully understand. And so might you relinquish all you believe this day, all you have used as your foundational footing as that understanding that is all about knowing what might be in a space of not knowing? And so enlist now to not know once again.

Enlist now to know something more deeply, more fully, more completely in the space where you now reside. Do so by resetting the subconscious, doing the self-guided meditation where you release beliefs, doing some process that you will let your entire being know that it is time to shake it up. To shake it up and to allow more to become known by you. More to become known in that it is time to un-know what you think you may know. It is as simple as that.

It is allowing from the space of not predetermining what each thing might be, what it might mean, what it is, from a pure premise of allowing more to be in existence this day. Allow more to be in existence this day as you move to yield what you do not presuppose to know by relinquishing and releasing all that is in current play.

Do you see it is a shaking up? It is a re-posturing. It is an allowing for the alignment to be held, and done, and occur differently. It is the pure potentiality of allowing more to be known, to eradicate and erase those things that have come before. Those things that have seemingly taken you off target. Those things that have taken you on a joy ride, so to speak. But sometimes, it is not in a joyous manner. Sometimes it is in a more beleaguered, and belabored, and problematic way. Because the mind does twist, and turn, and postulate, and formulate all that has come before. And the subconscious does store much of this within its groove, within its un-forgetting, unrelenting posture to protect. Do you see that oftentimes that which you believe to be familiar and feels right is something that is from a collective way, something you have carried with you for a time, and another time, and more time?

And now we say to shake the dust from your feet. To shake the lingering inability to connect as before. We say to re-posture, reformulate, and look again with refreshed eyes. To see things from a manner of knowing there is more.

Knowing there is more awaiting your fresh eyes to look upon it all again.

Do so this day. Reset the subconscious. Reformulate, look again, and re-posture. Do so with refreshed and renewed eyes. Do so from a revitalized perspective. Do so as in the wonderment of the child. Do so looking upon each thing as you might with those fresh eyes that do not see what was before them, before.

Now look upon each thing and recognize that it was there for a purpose, but it was a bit askew. It was a bit adjacent to rather than in alignment with what you sought. And so when it was adjacent, and you drifted in that direction, you moved away from that which needed to be aligned with. And we just seek to move you back on course. To move you back to that point where more can transpire. And in that transgression of transgression-airy posture, and in that mode of moving, and transpiring from this to that, and aligning differently, you can then move in a way that does result as you prefer.

And so we ask this day for you to align as never before. To shift and move and to allow this reset of the subconscious to shift-change you. To move you to want to enact life differently. To allow things to drop from you, premises, or predispositions that are no longer necessary. And that now when you move, you will do so in a cleaner, clearer, less-encumbered way — a less-encumbered state of mind, a less-encumbered formulation of flow.

This is what we wanted you to know. That this is an important step. This is most diligently sought. And we seek for you to know it, to do it, and to align this way as never before.

Chapter 3

Your Earthbound Adventure

As we begin, consider this. Consider the vastness of all that is, and how it has come together, all these things to progress from this space, from this Earth plane. To have all the tools, all the necessities, all the things that necessitate a successful outcome of this earthbound adventure.

And if you recognize that there is no time in that space from which you came.

And that time is illusionary and is felt here so uniquely. Then do you recognize how each thing is as it is for a purpose? That you have this opportunity to feel, and to do, and to experience that which you did not know before becoming earthbound. That which you did not know before entering this Earth plane. And so you have a true connectedness in all that is from the posture and the premise that these things were unknown previously.

They may have been supposed or believed to be a certain way, but there was not the actual understanding of it, fully, until there was an entrance into this dimension. And so we would say that this dimension is uniquely, aspirationally, intentionally, as it is, so that there is the full weightiness, there is the full understanding, there is the full proclivity to know that which was unknown before.

And so even in the drama of it, even in the midst of being amid all that is, there is, we will say, a beauty in it. For it is uniquely yours and uniquely an experience which will be intrinsic to your Soul's understanding of all that is. All that is before you now. And all that is in play.

If you look at this as your Soul might, for this unique experience and how this personality does walk this Earth, does take form, human form, in order to experience what is in this dimensionality of life. And so, do recognize there is an intrinsic gift and value given to the Soul experience that you experience. But there are some that have been in this platform, and in this performance, and in this game, in this reality for quite some time.

And we would say there is a lessening and the illusion becomes more permanently felt, but we would say this is illusionary also. But when you are in the midst of it all, when you are in the drama of it all, when you are in the throws of all that is, there is the firmly felt belief that this is real. And it is not. It is that which it is, but it is not permanent, and there is no permanence to it.

Each knows they will pass from the screen of life in a time they are unaware of, whether by illness or another intent of the drama of the activity of this, which we will call your life. And know when it is time to progress from here to there, there will be an occurrence that will take one from here to there. And so do not get stuck in the midst of the muck of the day.

Do not get stuck in all that is, that does out-picture itself, for at some point you must buoy yourself beyond all that does out-picture itself in a most significant way here. And so we will say to align in the premise that you are a visitor from afar and you want to experience and know how this or that feels.

And when you have gotten to that understanding, and you know exactly how it feels, and you say this does not feel good, or it does not feel as I would prefer it to feel, or have assumed it to feel, or had laid claim to the belief of how this or that felt, but now I know more personally that it is not something I wish to experience, but I wish to experience the full totality of what lay in its converse. Then, you move with more purpose to enact that thing because you know what it is not. And now you move toward what it is. And what might be experienced and the expansiveness that exists there. Do you see this? Do you recognize there is more for you to align, and do, and be?

So shake off the dust from your clothing. Shake off the unreality which has layered and lofted about you. And that you move in step to all that does wait illumination. Does wait to be out-pictured and seen from the expansiveness where it lay dormant in waiting.

And we will say each thing is just within reach, just within your grasp. And so we ask now for you to remove the mental limitation. Remove that mental box of knowingness. And do see how you can now place it on the shelf, for a time, as we discourse further. For there is much which we wish to share, but we will limit and share small kernels that are more palatable at this point.

And so as man came into form, and as man progressed in time, the diminishment of all that is known evaporated just a bit. Evaporated and was not as prevalently understood as before. And we would say that there is the proclivity, there is the understanding, there is the lack thereof, of so many small details that have become eclipsed. Those that have been minimized and eradicated, erased, removed, for they are not seen.

And when something is not seen, it is unknown until there is the pausing and the formulation for what was … not; to be moved into place, and into experiential aspects of being, when one does focus and draw that which is submerged, so to speak, and below the surface.

We seek for you to do just that. For you to focus upon what is not seen, not known, not recognized, except for the feeling component that you can lay claim to. That you can pause, and meditate, or consciously envision what is not yet known for your lifestream.

As you pause in meditation, or in a

meditational way, you can pull up those aspects that are just below the surface that are unseen at this time, but that await entry. You can draw forth energetic gifts that are yours to lay claim to from other undertakings in other times. You can draw these into your awareness this day. You can take in and understand all that does wait to express itself from a component of wonderment and awe. It is in the imagination that many (of these) can be assessed and accessed.

Do pause the mental gravity of the moment. Do pause the mental wonderment and exploratory nature of wanting to so define what will be said and move it off and away from further examination. Lay claim to more. Lay claim to more that is and awaits discovery now.

For we will say that when you pause, you might also elicit a posture through perhaps a small verse that does in rhythm and flow, allow you to engage because it will be a key of sorts. And you can take this and utilize it word for word. Or you can customize it as it does shift and change energetically with the insertion of other words, which may slightly change its rhythm and flow, but will work more intrinsically for you than this entry verse may in time.

And we would say it will go like this …

Shift-Change Verse

We seek for you to discover and find
what is key to discern and define.
Know through Light and Love,
all things can flow from up above.
Encircle your life force with only those things
designed to reinforce.

You see, you are all you need to be
within this vast Earth density.
But as your true purpose awaits discovery,
seek a means of rapid recovery.
It is why you came here; it is why you remain here.
So enlist a means of connection in this time.

You knew it originally for you sought it to be
because you wanted to understand something
more vividly.
But you needed this density, and it's become quite clear
that it's time to enact what has always remained near.

Shift-Change Verse
(continued)

And so begin from the heart center, start from this space.
Begin in this way to facilitate haste.
Access this most valued resource to navigate a new course,
    so all might become known and engaged.

For over time it was lost, not seen for you see,
    when you cannot see something so vividly.
It's hard to recall, hard to know why you want it at all,
    but it was the means to understand more over time.

And so know now this as you seek to uncover each veiled gift,
    and the messages they sought to impart.
Start in Light and Love this day,
    to engage and put into play,
    what you seek in an unending way.

When you engage as suggested, consciously moving into cue,
    all you sought to behold for it was then you knew,
    by keeping mental thoughts at bay, throughout the day,
    all could be enacted in a most expeditious way.

How to Customize Your Verse

Discovery of what you seek is the key,
  so reframe each verse to shift in time
    based on your mastery.
Free the little small voice who awaits and wants to say
    how each thing can align in a most magical way.

Keep the beat and rhythm,
    so you might align with what's best
    to move forward over time to engage all the rest.
Enlist a moving connection, and this is key,
      for all that's in play to now formulate and be.

Chapter 4

Your Original Incarnation & Its Original Purpose

To consider life to be anything other than what it is — the magnificent marvel of all that might be created and made manifest — would be to diminish that which is. For you see, so much is determined by what the mind will allow to come through the portal, and pathway, and entrance into this world of form.

And so you see, often, there is a picking and choosing of what might be best to formulate upon. And we would say that this is a most weighty matter, for there is much speculation and disagreement as to why thus and such is so. And we will say that it could be because of your upbringing. It could be because of genetics. It could be for a myriad of reasons, but we would say you must ultimately take control of the mental vessel so you can move in a proximity, and a pathway, of the things you preferred to discover once long ago.

And there are many that are in embodiment who have been doing just that — embodying — for quite some time. And those we have reached out to in numerous platforms and methodologies to enlist that they then remember. That they remember what they set about to understand so long ago.

And so we will say this chapter deals with your original purpose. That purpose you crafted when you first took embodiment into form so you might understand, in an energetic way, how this or that would feel rather than as it might be in textbook or in a textbook-like understanding.

For you see, so often there is the posturing and belief of this or that, and Earth has been and will remain for a time a schoolroom of sorts, where one can step into form to understand more fully what this or that might truly be. And how it might feel to enact this or that, or to create and to emblazon some understanding, and how it would feel from the accomplishment of the undertaking, and the recognition of all that is set into motion from the posture of doing.

And some may believe this purpose is a thing, but really the thing is the byprod-uct of that which you energetically strive to understand. If you look at it that you can create and do most anything when you have the wonderment of all that is, and no restriction from the mind placed upon you, then you can see so much more can flow into formation. And then it is no longer in flux and flow but actually affixed and made more real by the enactment of it.

And so, move this day to understand what that purpose was so long ago. And we will say that in the in-between time and in subsequent embodiments, there have been life purposes for those incarnations. But we will also say that they are not the full expansive preference to know, do, or be in those subsequent times.

For each time the transitory time did take place, there was a degree of stepping down from that overarching premise that was first crafted. For how can it be that you would know as much from one embodiment to the next? And perhaps there is a greater understanding in one or a lesser understanding. But each one, as you moved into that in-between time, did reflect the understanding that was held when last embodied.

When that life plan was crafted and made for the subsequent incarnation, there was the understanding as it related to that specific life. For in that life, there may have been a buoying up, or not, of that being. And so if there was a successful encounter in that lifetime and there was more that was understood and gleaned, then the subsequent incarnation did reflect that, for there was more crafted perhaps into what was sought to be understood. But we would say that the overall understanding of what was wanted was not the full understanding of what was initially conceived.

Recognize this and know each thing is as it is meant to be. And because we have also shared that there are dual lifetimes in play today, dueling for supremacy and to achieve the outcome, perhaps, more quickly — but also, perhaps, more in tune with what is, then we will say there is another component at play here.

And so will you be receptive to receive that there is another dimension where it is almost a mirroring aspect where other lifetimes are also enacted? Where other realities are in play because other choices exist where another outcome may be perceived or wanted, for they are unique and separate occurrences and not exact mirror replicas of one to the other.

So there may be a completely different dimension going on concurrently with many of the same players to see the outcome that is derived in that understanding. And so this is a stretch of the imagination. This is a stretch of the understanding which may be in play within your own dynamic. But we would say to consider this as well, for it does have an overarching contribution to the mix that is in play today.

And so when you are in meditation, might you consider to connect to this parallel adventure? If you will do so, then you can see and feel if you are buoyed up, or not, in this other existence. And if there is a buoying up, might you consider tethering this existence to that one? So that if there is a means of reinforcement, if there is a means of advancement, if there is a means of drawing the energy from one to the other because you have wanted it to be so by your focused intention and your attention to it, then you can redirect some of that energy to you now.

We do want you to pause and to sit with this for a time. So that you might draw in that which you perceive, that which you now consider, and that which now is in play.

❧ *Contemplative Pause* ❧

And now that you have played in the energy that we have introduced, we ask you to continue to explore and to return often. And maybe refresh these words so that they might become renewed with you.

And you might say, *perhaps I am the one that others prefer to tarry with and tether to.* And this may be so. Then it is up to you to seek to connect with them. And you can do so by stilling the mind and allowing what may enter into it as you look at the vistas that are before you. Do you see one that is struggling, that seeks to connect with you, or unknowingly exists without the understanding of the tethering process? And so is it worthwhile then for you to seek the connection? And we would say, yes, because this is an aspect of your Soul and ultimately of you.

As you look upon life this day, do see it in a uniquely marvelous way. Because there are things you may not have known about before, yet have always existed. And so can you see when you tether and fortify another, you then buoy yourself up to a degree? Because you have enlisted steps to help another. And in that assistance, you can be so much more because now you are a lifeline to the other. And you will reinforce, and engage, and be able to bring forward that which may not have reached the level that you now exist in. And so, look at life in its wonderment. Look at life and the opportunities you represent, and that you have become aware of, so that you might be more in all that you do, all that you enact, and all today you know to be.

Chapter 5

Now That You Know

Now that you know, do you see how so much more is and does exist within life? Within the totality of all that you might do and be, do you see that as you seek more, more is given? As you yearn for an understanding and saw negativity and things that were not preferred in your past, can you look again? Can you look again and see the gift that was given? If not then, perhaps now? For in the recognition of the gift that had been there all along, you then look upon life in its totality in a different way. You look seeking to know what the gift is. You look in wonderment and awe, and with the quizzical nature of the child. Do you see that this is, as it is, for a purpose?

For if you readily saw each, then there would not be the mystery attached to the gift. And isn't the gift a bit mysterious when it is wrapped and disguised so that the full extent of what is inside that wrapped gift is not immediately known?

Can you look at life in this way? Can you look at life in the wonderment of all that it is? Can you see life exudes, and portrays, and emits almost an energy of wonderment, of possibility, of all that seeks to become known in the portal and the pathway that you've created?

The portal is the opening and the opportunity to see what was not seen. And the pathway is the means by which you travel to get to where you seek to go. And when you know each thing given does hold a key, a key to what you could not see without its added measure, then you look upon this gift differently.

You look upon it when you are ready to do so, with a bit of quizzical wonderment. And we have said it is the wonderment of a child. And so when you look, always knowing that life would never serve you that which is not for your betterment; is not for your discovery of knowing what it is, and then being able to implement it once the awareness has entered in. For you see, if you remain in the neediness and the less-than energy, you may never connect to the other.

And so know that this day: that the gift is truly a gift. And it is all that it needs to be, and it is in the awareness and recognition of what it is and needs to be seen to be, by you, for you to advance, in a manner of speaking, to the next level of play. And so know this as we proceed.

Gifts Given

And so, gifts present themselves in a variety of ways. And you may not see them as a gift. But know they exist in this guise none-theless. If you have a course correction, if you have perhaps a calamity or some other issue has caused you to be and become perplexed, can you pause and look at it differently?

We would say when you still the mind and look from the quizzical aspect of a child, you can see what is more clearly before you and what has truly been given. It is another opportunity to see life in a different way. And so when you posture and determine that you want to see life differently, and you are willing to relinquish the belief system that you have held, then you can adopt and even adapt to new opportunities and things which were always present, yet presently unknown.

And these are nothing new. They have been invoked and utilized in previous times, but they are remaining dormant at this time. And if there are some who have discovered their methodology, then perhaps they might listen in, too, to see if they might expand what they know.

And so, you can formulate, and postulate, and imagine a variety of things. And each of those things have the potentiality to become real, to become known, to become a part of your day and put into play.

When you envision them, focus upon them for a time and then release them to only reengage them later to stir them up, so to speak. To revive what you have planted as a seed. It is as if you were watering what you had planted. And so look upon each thing as the gift that it is. Look upon each thing when you move out of the angst of the mind, or the perplexities of the situation, to engage and to think of it once again, in a new way; in a way in which you might not have considered before.

Today, let us talk briefly about something that is perhaps new on the horizon, and, perhaps not. But it is how to posture and formulate more. And so when you consider that you have a hearing disability or perhaps a ringing in the ear, do you stop and say, *Hmm? What has caused this nuance? Why is this at my door?* If, however, you engage with this new addition to your life in fear, anxiety, and a bit of mayhem, that (mayhem) might develop in time.

For you see, when mayhem is introduced, or thought about, or there are perplexities that are felt, then you are not seeking a true resolve to the situation. But, rather, something that might be medically induced to subside the symptoms. But the symptoms are simply there to let you know that you need to look into this or that in a most whimsical way.

And so this day, there was such an occurrence. And the thought was at that point, *Hmm ... am I to look differently at this ringing in my ear? Why is this happening? And what might I do to alleviate it? Might I search for something that will allow me to hear insights and messages, perhaps, differently than I had before?* And that was exactly the right posture to engage and perceive.

And so do you see when you look at each (occurrence or situation) with a quizzical understanding, a quizzical way, a quizzical mental engagement, then you do not engage the fear aspect but the whimsy and wonderment of the child. And so, yes, there are other ways to engage that which seeks to share insights from another dimension. And oftentimes it introduces itself and sounds very much as the mental mind does. And so there is a degree of discernment which must be maintained, at all times, so that ego does not enter in and take you off-course.

And this can be rather perplexing over time when you begin to question each and every new insight because it is new. And it is not something that you've heard before. And how do you know if it is true, or not, unless you delve within and sit with it in contemplation, to know if this or that is correct or true? And so if there is another means where you can, almost like an on-off switch, turn on a means to (almost) hear the messages a bit differently.

We would say that you must resonate with what is given so you have that inner discernment to know if it is true. But we will also say there is a degree of distinction that can also be given so that you can determine what is what, and who is who.

And so this is what we seek to engage you with this day so that you might have more ingredients to put into the mix and that might make things a little bit easier to digest. As you look to understand and discern this insight, seek to still your mind once again, and then we will … continue.

∞ *Meditational Pause* ∞

And so we seek now for you to become and be, all that you might be. When insights present themselves that do not align with you as you might anticipate, sit with the premise for a time so that it might integrate, and you might receive it differently. These are signs and ways for you to look upon life so that not only might you integrate, but you may not, at this point, miss the greater objective. And the greater objective is to align you with all you seek, move you into that space of readiness, and to adopt then a posture that will move you to all that is.

For there is much that awaits your discovery and much that will move you

— differently. Differently than you have moved in this lifetime, perhaps, but not in previous ones. For you have soared to great heights and done things unimaginable in the densities which exist here.

For from here to there, there is a great gulf, and this is maya and illusion. And the illusionary posture from which you now reside seems most dense, heavy, weighted as you fully feel this life experience, which is how it is meant to be. For you to not want an experience which is unbelievable, do you? Of course not. You want to be in the fullness of it. You want to be at the forefront of it. You want to be in the midst of it.

And so that is where you find yourself today. You find yourself in the midst of this or that drama, this or that activity, this or that undertaking, and it seems oh so diffi-cult to move from here to there. And so we say now, release all of that, and know that you are Pure Essence at your core. You reside currently in this physical form for the exponential opportunity to experience what you did not understand before.

We seek to give you other tools, but you must be receptive for them. And knowing that you have not known of them perhaps in this lifetime, or maybe several others. But it is time. It is time and past time. And as you see, in another illusionary way, that sometimes there is that thing that is ready to take off, soar, and fly. But you are not there. You miss, say, the boat. Or, in this case, an airplane trip. As you go through what you have and need and find that your papers are missing. These papers are most important for they are your flight pass, your boarding pass, your ability to embark and engage in that next leg of your journey. And so what to do? What to do? *What to do …* ?

Again, we say to place that mental box upon the shelf as we seek to elaborate and extol. For you see, there is a means and methodology you might enlist. It is something you can do which is similar to perhaps what you have heard before of an on-off switch which we have just mentioned. But we would say there is more to it than that.

And so, as you look to engage what might allow for another portal of under-standing, another pathway of promise to be communicated, be sure to put that mental box upon the shelf, again. We would say one more time, but we know within this life there will be many opportunities for which you will want to do the exact same thing. And that is to place that mental box upon the shelf.

It is that you have to recognize when it is time to do so. And just to allow the words to permeate and fall over your form … as rain would fall upon you, and then the water becomes absorbed by your skin. It is that absorption we seek. It is that opportunity to allow it to shower you, to transcend the mental blocking that might occur other-wise. For the mind does block what it does not accept. And so place that mental box (on the shelf) now and let us begin again.

For you see there is an on-off switch that does reside in your mental awareness, but might you allow more to be known this day? Yes, take a deep breath as you see the mental box placed upon the shelf.

Take a deep breath in. And let it out. In … and out … in … and out …

❧ Pause to Breathe Deeply Now ❧

Meditation

There are many portals and pathways, as we have alluded to, that are unseen. They are unseen, and so there must be that space that you prepare for them; that open space, mentally. That cavity you now see hollowed out because the box has been removed … temporarily. And you might see an on-off switch that you might now flip on. Then, keep walking in this hollowed area, and might we say also, hallowed area.

And as you move into the proximity of being from your heart center, combine the heart and the head together. See a melding of the two, almost a swirling, as there is an integration of heart and head, as you place your hands over the heart space.

Feel the integration, as you feel the heartbeat that does now proceed as we progress into this knowing. And so, you have turned on the switch. And you feel the beating of your heart. And you know all is right within the world in which you reside. All is safe in the pureness, and the holiness, and the Loving aspect which you find yourself feeling, and conveying out into the world. Stay in this space for a mere few moments, and then we will continue.

◈ *Meditational Pause* ◈

Tether, align, anchor with all there is. Complete a figure-eight formation which begins from the heart, and energetically encircle that which you seek. And so here we seek to know that which is beyond this life force. And we have spoken of those who are in existence in a mirrored sort of way. Those that are also a part of the Soul Essence, which is also connected and gives life to this body. And so seek to know, and hear, and understand that one that is in many ways a part of you.

And as we have discussed, may be of a higher or lower calibre. And so let us say perhaps they are of a higher calibre and you want to tether to them. But you also want to seek to communicate, discuss, and hear what they have to say at many times throughout the day. Or when you are in this posture of Loving embrace, tethering, and seeking to know more — seeking to be illumined. For as we have said, when a teacher is needed, one will appear. And is it so unusual to believe that teacher might be from within, or out, but still a part of this same Soul Essence?

And so, seek to know more. Seek to recognize more, but let us give you a pathway in which to do so. As you still the mind, focus on a figure-eight formation which connects the two together. In your mind's eye, now that you have created that space and you have the on-switch in the on position, tether now from the head to the heart with a figure-eight flow of energy.

Also, then conjecture a figure-eight flow of energy from that same heart space out into that mirrored aspect. And perhaps, the third tethering to your unseen Entourage of Light and Love so all are in accordance and rotating and vibrating together, maintaining that the mental box now is still placed upon the shelf.

And so, now, as you sit in this contemplative mode, tethering, and anchoring these things, might you then elicit questions and discernments that will formulate and flow back to you? And as we began this discussion, what about discerning between what you hear, and perhaps ego entering in, or something that is not quite of the vibration that you intend to give the answers that you seek?

As you imagine and see the energy in-flow, now let us move to the last ingredient as you enter and sprinkle Love into all that is. As you add Universal Love to the components that are in play, you see a swirling and a melding as all three figure-eight flows intertwine once more.

Now seek to hear with a discerning eye *(stet)*. With a discernment that is placed upon you from the knowledge of all that is, is proceeding through Light and Love. All that is given is given in this way. And as you grow to do this exercise more routinely, you will hear more distinctly what is given. And it will be from a space of discernment and understanding.

You might even ask to define what you hear in a different way other than your own voice. So what is forthcoming might be uniquely and distinctly received in a manner that is most immediately discernible from who the source is. And we ask for you to practice with this now for a mere few moments, and then we will add just a bit more to complete this thought process and this methodology.

❧ Meditational Pause ❧

Now that you have stored the mental loop, the mental box on the shelf, and perhaps even locked that frequency, or done some other endeavor that maximizes the ability for the mental knowingness to stay disengaged … now, we will begin anew.

Seek to elicit a posture of Love. Seek

from all that is to begin from the heart center, from the heart space, as you again engage the figure-eight flow into the mental space where the mental box did reside once before.

See this figure-eight flow as pure energy. See it rev up as a light that beams within the energy of the figure-eight flow. See the sequence and the flowing from one to the next, from that to the other as it does speed up, and the momentum does increase until it is a solid beam of light. And when this movement becomes a solid white light of energy, allow for the maximization of this charge to set in. And set the intention that now you have engaged in a new space.

And see, then, the other figure-eight formations you have created, moving in the same manner where they then seemingly become this solid white light. This light does then anchor and move down with you in an energetic way, to the center of the Earth as you release the anchoring that is there. And now you float freely from these three points of light and emerge in a brilliance of wonderment and awe.

See Universal aspects, stars, and constellations. See all that is melding and entering your line of vision. And now ask those questions which you need addressed. Ask those questions now that you are untethered, in any other way, except to these. And now seek to hear the answers, defining how you wish to hear them. If in a specific way, or tone, or something that is uniquely designed for you to know that you have aligned as you preferred. Seek this now, to play in the wonderment of all that is and to know that more can now be.

❧ *Meditational Pause* ❧

~ Might more now be … ~

Chapter 6

In Readiness, All Will Grow

Do you see that often in life, you are met with adversity, which is a cloaked gift in disguise? For if you moved in the direction or continued in the pathway that you had planned, you would not be, perhaps, where you are today. Because different things became introduced, and you had to change the manner in which you were moving.

This is what we want you to focus upon today and each day moving forward. As you move and grow, you must look always, unceasingly, in a conscious sort of way, to know what other gifts and avenues are available. For if you would routinely stop, we would suggest that so would much of the adversity that comes to your door.

For when you are in a reflective state, when you are in a state of whimsical wonder, and looking at life and what you have accomplished, and what this day or that day might have been or will be, but not in a less-than energy but in a whimsical wonderment sort of way, pausing to posture how this or that might be best, you can see if you are exactly where you intended to be, or somewhere else.

So if you will do these measures, not invoking a lesser energy, not bringing forward a needy, less-than posture, then you will see that you can discover much. For it is in the posturing and the *perhaps* mode of life that you can discover what you need to discover — what Universe seeks for you to discover. What you might embrace as opposed to having some calamity befall you, some disease enter in, something other than that which you prefer because you did not stop to look otherwise.

And do you see, it is the stopping and looking and wondering that might allow for a different set of circumstances to cross your path? For now you are looking for what might be the betterment of your life. And so when you look in the wonder of all that is, when you look from the Loving posture of all that is given, then you will more easily see what is available to be seen and awaits recognition. And wouldn't that be a better way to go than to have some this or that happen within your future that is not desired?

And so, too, know that life is meant to be one of change. And when people pass from the screen of life, there is a need for almost a celebration of the life that was led. The time they were with you, the opportunities you shared, and the intrinsic things that will never pass from this screen of life or from your memory. And isn't that a better way to envision than one of loss? For don't you want what is best for the one who has made their transition?

Don't you want what they want from a life that perhaps no longer offers them the value, or perhaps has already offered the value that they sought? And now it is time to move on to other objectives and other things. And so will you stop the pity party, in many ways, of those things that you have learned to embrace from a less-than level? And know that life is as it is, in a manner of speaking, because each has their own objective which you may or may not know.

For how can you know what one has set up prior to embodiment? How can you know what they knew on the inner and perhaps not in the outer? And that would suppose that you have greater knowledge, perhaps, than you do. And so release them. Release them in the joy and the wonderment of what they have discovered and are soon to discover in their next embodiment or next undertaking. Isn't that a better way to be? For life is not meant to be static, and all are not meant to stay within this life. And so many are stuck at this point. And we would say to move on, for they have moved on, and it is time for change.

Trigger, Ignite, Remember

Now we move to our next topic. And we move on to those things which we seek your attention to understand. And again, to place that mental box up upon the shelf so that it does not distract, it does not interpret, and it does not enter in where there is no use for this mental box.

We also stress within this life that you, oftentimes when trying to interpret or understand, just let the words permeate your form. Permeate your form and allow all to become intertwined and immersed in the waters that shower you with Love and information. And in many ways there is a remembering that is also triggered. In this way, you are allowing a triggering to have time to ignite. For that remembering to become unfettered; to rise up and be integrated in your general awareness once again.

And so you cannot take Heaven by storm. You cannot rush things when you are not in the position to rush them. And ego often is the culprit here that wants things quickly. Wants it right now! Doesn't want to wait! Wants to make sure that things continue to move!

But do you see that when you slow the pace, when you take a breath and breathe, that you are in a measure, and a manner of speaking, allowing? You are in a measured way of allowing more to be in your life this day. And isn't that preferred? That you recognize all that is in existence, and all that waits, and awaits your recognition?

When you consider and can see it this way, isn't that a wondrous thing? To take in life and this life, and all the beauty that does surround you when you can recognize the more that does exist and awaits your wanting to connect with it.

And so, we do greet you this day in the wonderment of all that is. In the wonderment and knowledge that life is, and offers all that you seek for it to be. And all you seek to know is available when you enlist the right tools, the right understanding in shifting your perspective to allow what you may not have considered before to be in the forefront of all that is this day.

The Importance of Your Original Purpose

When you seek to enact an objective, perhaps your life intention, your purpose, your reason for being in the nowness of this space, what thing might you do? How might you progress it, to make it manifest, sooner rather than later?

And why is there an importance here?

Why is there an importance here?

Why is there an importance here?

And we would say that it is the reason you have come into embodiment. It is the reason you have chosen to be in this Earth space. It is the reason you came and embodied to understand some thing that you did not understand when Pure Essence … when you were Consciousness in Flow.

Do you see that this thing you wanted to understand was an energy that you needed to take time to fully immerse in? So that you understood the intrinsic nature of what it is you wanted to experience and know.

And so you are here on this planet so you might understand what this energy, perhaps emotional energy, is. And to fully understand it, there must be the converse of it. And so there is that push-pull dynamic of understanding the lesser aspect before you can know the full capacity of the greater one.

This is why you came into embodiment. This is why you came into embodiment in your first incarnation. It was to know more specifically, more personally, how it felt and what it was to be in that energy. But perhaps coming into the densities of Earth, and its schoolroom, in many regards, was more difficult and more cumbersome than that one had known in spiritual form.

And so when they passed from that life into the in-between time, they found they were not able to experience that which they sought to understand. And so another life was crafted, a similar objective was put into play, known as their purpose, and they then embodied once again. But this time, there was not the fuller dynamic of that initial understanding, which was preferred. Let us say it was a minimization of what was first crafted. And this has continued over time. Each time, utilizing the life from which they evolved from to formulate and craft the next life.

And if there was a misfortune, a lesser understanding or embodiment, and perhaps even a most difficult one, when exiting that life, there would not be the full expanse of wonderment and awe to enact another life that would be better. Perhaps there was a belief that there is difficulty here on this Earth, and . . . *If I could just do thus and such, and this and that, that would be enough.* Or perhaps, *if I could enact more difficulty, then I would know more* and many other misconstrued perspectives. But never quite getting to the overarching, all-encompassing, original purpose that was postured when coming from Pure Essence, from Spirit, into physical form.

And so now, after many incarnations, there has been a degree of digressing, a degree of lessening, a degree of *not all there is* to the equation and to the components of this puzzle. And so we seek to enlighten to the fact that you did have this original mission. This original mission was what you wanted to understand, coming from

Spiritual Essence into the densities of the Earth plane. And they have not been understood to the level you set out to have them be understood.

And now you are in the midst of the maya of the day. And the maya is quite illuminating in that it illuminates so much that is in play today. You see it with illness, with plague, with death, with destruction, with all of those things that are not preferred. And they do exist in some form or fashion in every embodiment in which you have lived.

And you may take on a cause, and you may believe this cause is the most important thing that you must help to right a wrong. But do you know, and might you know, that in every lifetime there are many causes for which you can fly the flag, take up the banner, become involved? And that is not a bad thing to do. It is a good thing to move in step with righting a wrong. But we would say that, and we would hope that you would say that it is time to roll up your sleeves to get about why you are here. To get about why you have continued to incarnate on this Earth.

And it is quite simply because you have become lost in the maya that does exist here. And perhaps you believe you have discovered all you need to know because you have received inner confirmation that you have discovered all there is. And now you just need to ride out your time so you can find out that what you know is so.

You see, in this space, the illusionary is not real. And there is the belief that all that has been gleaned was exactly right and so. And then you go about planning the next incarnation and living that life. We will say that this time is not as you might believe it to be. This time is not as it appears. And you are being reinforced by what you believe to be true, as opposed to what is. For Universe seeks to make you right. Universe seeks to reinforce all you believe to be so, even when it is not. Even when what you believe to be true is the illusion you believed while embodied.

And so, ask questions in this in-between time. If you choose not to shift or change at this point, and that is fine to do, or not. But we would say to always ask questions, and to not be relegated to do this or that in an expedient way but to pause, and to question, and to ask, for we will say within this life, you cannot know all, for you are not in the space to know all because you have the mind which enters in to block and interpret.

And within each life, there is that sort of awareness that does enlist to be of assistance. But over time, it has been allowed to rule your vessel. And what we suggest here is you regain the controls. You utilize the mind and ego in their appropriateness and when it is appropriate to do so. But not to allow the controls to be taken over by that which is not consciously aware.

And so, seek this day to connect once again to your original purpose. Seek this day to know the overarching objective that your Soul had to embody on this planet long ago. Seek to know and recognize your purpose in this life is a component of that. It is a component simply because it cannot be all that it was originally because each lifetime there was not the remembering of the original one.

Recognize your original purpose is that which is the all-encompassing rationale and reason for your being here in this space. And you have gotten lost in all the objectives and causes that have turned your head and caused you to embrace that which will always need a measure of attention.

And we would say your original purpose could be a component of what you are already doing, but it is from the awareness postured when you attach to that which was the reason for your being. And when you engage from that level and from that perspective, then you look upon the occurrence differently.

So it may be this thing you are already doing but perhaps not quite the way in which you need to enlist or look upon it. But by implementing a slight shift, you might be able to do just that.

Move this day and know your original purpose is why you chose to embody in that original lifetime, having placed before you an original purpose.

But we will say the contrast (or opposing element), sometimes, have taken those who embodied out of embodiment, for they did not see the gift in the contrast that was given. The contrasting and opposing element was not seen, visibly, by the one who needed to know that countermeasure. And they did not stop perhaps and pause to ask what it might be. But then did let life direct them, Universe direct them, by introducing this countermeasure. And had they embraced the countermeasure and recognized it for what it was, they would have chuckled and been grateful. But instead chose a different path and perhaps moved out of that embodiment and into that in-between time.

And so recognize this. Recognize there is more to life. There is more to what you sought. And isn't it time to know what you wanted to know, and has moved you to reembody, and experience what you could not understand in any other way?

About the Elders

Think upon Us as a Consciousness of Light and Love. Think upon Us as ever-moving light that does fluctuate and form words within the in-breath and out-breath of a beat or measure. Think upon Us as Love, in Love with all that is. We are Beings that wish for humanity to have answers that have eluded them in recent times. There are those who have shared such information, but it is also being released in this manner, in this time, so there might be a profound knowingness as one engages with life here. We are Pure Consciousness. We are many, and We provide insights for humanity so that more might be gleaned in this lifetime than without such knowledge. We are Love, but all are that which is.

About the Author

Robyn G. Locke bridges the physical with the nonphysical world to bring you purpose-driven, self-healing, self-help books. She is a transformation facilitator, gifted speaker, energy intuitive, and spiritual seeker. *Love life and even what appears to be bad. Discover the deeper meaning attached to each thing encountered along the way. Engage in life's mystery.*

Her inspirational writings are given by the Elders. They provide invaluable insights and suggest refreshingly simple steps to engage. Imagine your future when mental constructs are removed and replaced with purposeful direction. Unbounded opportunities await as you consciously co-create all you desire to manifest.

Discover more at
www.AdvancedEnergetics.org

Find Our Books

BOOK ONE

The Little Book to Find Your Purpose
WHEN ALL ALIGNS FOR YOU

What's the point without purpose? Do you seek inner fulfillment and yearn to discover more? Perhaps now is the time to:

- Learn more about the energy you are meant to enact and manifest here
- Discover the true value of Universal Love and how it can magically transform your life
- Recognize the significance of free will and why it's important to feel each experience created
- Understand how thoughts create feelings, and feelings create emotions bringing forth actions or reactions which result in your manifested reality
- Take steps to still and slow the mind; you are not your thoughts
- Produce better days when enlisting positive thoughts to replace those that don't feel good
- Release limitations and the negative what ifs of life as you engage in the positivity of what is now in play
- Find your roadmap to success, good health, and happiness as you consciously co-create all you desire and so much more

This *Little Book* provides fundamental and foundational knowledge for your platform of understanding. Universal Love is more keenly described so that you might move it into use today. Assimilate its intrinsic components, the means to still the mind, and the significance of your emotions.

BOOK THREE

Enact Your Purpose

Then Reach for the Stars

Discover a powerful means of transformation through compelling and thought-provoking guidance.

Tired of the mind games? Is it time to outwit the wit? Are you intrigued by what could lie outside the physicality of what you can more readily see and touch?

Enact Your Purpose was intuitively given to assist seekers to become more consciously aware and connected to what has been lost over time. With each understanding given, you'll draw new measures into action, redirect mental distractions, and unearth the deeper meaning of emotions. In this intriguing exploration of purposeful discovery, Locke bridges the physical with the nonphysical world and relates loving teachings that will gently guide you to pursue profound insights and change the way you see your life and this world.

In *Enact Your Purpose*, you'll discover:

- The steps to see past the endless mental banter as you understand why you are not your thoughts
- Energetic keys to elevate your frequency and help you to unlock the underlying premise of your purpose
- Effective ways to enact change as you implement some simple steps that will transform your existence, revolutionize how you see this life, and much, much more!

Enact Your Purpose is an invaluable resource to help you on your road to becoming satisfied and fulfilled. If you like thought-provoking guidance, mind-expanding knowledge easily implemented through simple instruction, and the means for transformative change, then you'll love Robyn G. Locke and the Elders' potent shift in perception.

136

Awaken
The Definitive Guide to Transformative Change

Do you have trouble manifesting what you want in life? Discover how to align your being and tap into those unlimited possibilities.

Feel like you're off-course? Hurdles stopping you in your tracks? Searching for guidance that seems no where to be found? Gifted speaker, change facilitator, and energy intuitive Robyn G. Locke conveys wisdoms given by the Elders – Beings of Pure Consciousness and Infinite Awareness. And now she's here to share powerful Universal insights to spark the means to enact a personal renewal of ultimate self-discovery.

Awaken: The Definitive Guide to Transformative Change is the must-have handbook for seekers desiring to co-create their best life. Its many exercises, relatable stories, meditational offerings, and other insightful approaches will help you release undesired negative energy and overcome those seemingly ever-present obstacles. Utilize new understandings and their platforms of possibility and promise as you relinquish self-limiting beliefs and discover new vistas.

In *Awaken*, you'll discover:

- How to easily, personally, and more readily transform your existence into one that manifests your dreams and desires
- Ways to unlayer and remove trapped emotional energy to help you shift-change into all you might be
- Instruction on the importance of your purpose and how you can step into this new pathway with confidence and ease
- Techniques that will self-heal, create wellness, and lead you to a more lasting happiness
- The ability to access inner fulfillment, shift-change your energy, see this life differently, and so much more

Awaken is an extraordinary resource accelerating the process of true inner awareness, restorative healing, and personal transformation. If you like enacting inspirational insights, garnering a deeper understanding of Universal Love's vast capabilities and timeless teachings, then get ready for the soul-stirring results these new discoveries will bring.

Are you ready to transform into more than your mind can currently fathom?

Connect with Us

Find us at

www.AdvancedEnergetics.org

Facebook: @AdvancedEnergetics

Instagram: @AdvancedEnergetics

Twitter: @theEldersListen

YouTube: AdvancedEnergetics

* 9 7 9 8 9 8 7 7 5 4 2 6 9 *